THE UNOFFICIAL
Hocus Pocus
COOKBOOK
for Kids

50 Fun and Easy Recipes for Tricks, Treats, and Spooky Eats Inspired by the Halloween Classic

BRIDGET THORESON

BLOOM BOOKS
FOR YOUNG READERS

Published by:
Bloom Books for Young Readers,
an imprint of Ulysses Press
PO Box 3440
Berkeley, CA 94703
www.ulyssespress.com

ISBN: 978-1-64604-545-7
Library of Congress Control Number: 2023938285

Printed in the United States by Sheridan Books Minnesota
10 9 8 7 6 5 4 3 2 1

Managing editor: Claire Chun
Project editor: Renee Rutledge
Proofreader: Barbara Schultz
Front cover and interior design: Winnie Liu
Artwork: Shutterstock.com except photos on pages 23, 25, 31, 47, 48, 52, 67, 83, 93, 101, 104, 107
    © Bridget Thoreson
Production: Jake Flaherty

To '90s kids, '90s kids at heart, and the kids of '90s kids.
And to Beatrice.

Contents

Introduction

It has been about 30 years since the film *Hocus Pocus* debuted (to a tepid welcome), and two years since I published *The Unofficial Hocus Pocus Cookbook*. In those two years, a great deal has happened in my world. *The Unofficial Hocus Pocus Cookbook* became a *USA Today* best-selling book, the movie *Hocus Pocus 2* premiered on Disney+ in the fall of 2022, and I became a parent for the first time.

The direct result of all these things is the book you are now reading. I had written *The Unofficial Hocus Pocus Cookbook* as an homage to a cult classic that I have loved since I was a child, that I rewatch multiple times every autumn, and for which I suspected—and then had resoundingly confirmed—that many, many other people have similar fond feelings. About a year after my cookbook was published, *Hocus Pocus 2* was released—and I, along with millions of other fans, could almost relive the first time I watched one of my favorite movies. *Hocus Pocus 2* was not *Hocus Pocus*—it never could be, coming 30 years later. But it was fun, it was clever, it was both pure and over the top, and it gave us more of the characters we love.

In between the day I submitted the manuscript for the first *Hocus Pocus* cookbook and when it was published, my daughter Beatrice was born. Of course, she is still too young to share a movie with me in any real way (particularly one that derives jokes from the idea of snacking on young children), but she was with me as I wrote the book and tested the recipes, as I did a small press tour, and as I watched other millennials like me relive their childhoods through the recipes and references in the book.

When we started talking about a follow-up project, my mind first went to Beatrice. I was excited for the day when she could watch the movie with me and share a part of my own life as a kid. I knew that many other millennial parents probably felt the same way, and so I knew I wanted to do a book that would enhance that experience. Not only could I share the movie with my daughter, but I could share the experience of cooking a recipe related to the movie. We could make Black Flame Pretzels or Petrified Spiders together in the kitchen, then sit down and snack while we watched the movie. I wanted to take the nostalgia of *The Unofficial Hocus Pocus Cookbook* and make it un-nostalgic, suitable for a new "batch" of children so that they might grow up and look back fondly on the movie for a different reason.

And so I wrote *The Unofficial Hocus Pocus Cookbook for Kids*. The recipes here are all friendly to a child's palette, and there's nothing that strays too far from the familiar. Many of the recipes can be prepared by children with a little adult supervision. Some require more active adult participation, while others could be achieved by even the smallest of hands.

As I wrote this book, I kept Beatrice in mind. She is 20 months old as I write this and has already started helping in the kitchen. She gets great pleasure from standing in her learning tower, chopping soft veggies with her child-safe knife. I believe that teaching her kitchen skills early on will not only prepare her to take care of herself throughout her life but will also give us strong shared experiences and lock in some core memories. If you're a parent, grandparent, aunt, uncle, godparent, or just an adult who has a special kid in your life, I hope this cookbook helps you to do the same. I hope it helps you to share two important things with that kid—a piece of yourself as a child, and a good meal!

In the "Torture Chamber"

How to Cook without an Ancient Spellbook

ADVICE FOR BEGINNERS—SAFETY FIRST

You might not have an all-seeing eye or ancient spellbook, but that doesn't mean you can't whip up some marvelous meals! But before you dive in, take a moment to think about kitchen safety. The kitchen is a fun and creative place, and it is important that you pay attention and keep it safe! Take a look at the following safety advice before heading into the kitchen to brew up a potion or bake a magical treat.

Talk to an adult before starting to make a recipe; they might have some advice for you. Let them look over the ingredients and tools you'll need to make sure you're set up for success. Cooking is a great thing to do as a family, so many of the recipes in this book are designed to work on together.

When in doubt, wash your hands! Wash your hands before cooking, after handling raw meat, after cutting smelly ingredients such as garlic, and after picking up something you dropped on the floor. Wash those hands!

Roll up your sleeves and pull back your hair. Long sleeves can get in the way and knock things over while you're cooking. They can also catch on fire if you're working over the stove! Be sure to roll your sleeves up so none of that happens.

Clean up after yourself. Cooking can get messy, and that's okay! But it's important to clean up any mess you've made. Or try cleaning as you cook so it isn't such a big task at the end.

Ask for help before you use a utensil for the first time. Pause and make sure you understand how it works and that you're doing things correctly. Sometimes you might feel like you've just woken from 300 years of sleep and nothing looks familiar. It's okay to ask for help.

9

Pay attention to hot surfaces. Keep towels (both paper and cloth), oven mitts, and pot-holders away from the stove.

Do your homework! Review the recipe directions and ingredient list before you begin. Take the time to gather and prepare all your ingredients.

Practice knife safety. Think SASS:

- **S**top—Pause and make sure no one is within arm's reach.

- **A**way—Cut away from your body and fingers, not toward them.

- **S**harp—A dull knife is dangerous! A sharp, clean knife is a safer knife. Ask an adult to check the knives before you use them and sharpen any that are dull.

- **S**tore—When you're done using a knife, put it away in a sheath or knife block.

Another thing to keep in mind is to always cut on a cutting board. Parents won't be pleased if their countertops suddenly look like they've been given a beating by an enchanted and particularly violent willow tree.

Wear closed-toe shoes. If you are just learning how to handle a knife, it's a good idea to wear closed-toe shoes just in case you accidentally drop the knife.

Never leave your cauldron unattended. If you're in the middle of cooking and need to leave the kitchen for some reason, turn off the stove. You can turn it on again when you get back.

SPELLS FOR EVERY LEVEL

I know not every witch has the same level of experience in the torture chamber—uh, kitchen—so I've marked each recipe's difficulty. If you are learning your way around the kitchen, focus on "Beginner" recipes and then work your way up. If you've already cast many successful kitchen spells, dive right in to the more complex "Advanced" recipes.

Beginner recipes don't require heat or major chopping; these are dishes little ones could do on their own, like the Fresh-Faced Cheese Platter (page 53). Children who already have basic skills can try "Intermediate" recipes, which require some cooking with heat and cutting ingredients but are generally uncomplicated and have fewer steps, such as Magicae "Mac"-xima (page 72). For kids who have more experience in the kitchen, advanced recipes will be more complex and require cooking techniques like deep frying, such as Newt Saliva and Fries (page 69).

 Beginner    **Intermediate**    **Advanced**

Common Recipe Terms

Al dente: Cooked just until firm—not crunchy and not too soft.

Bake: Cook in an oven using dry heat.

Baste: Add moisture to food while you're cooking it so that it doesn't dry out.

Beat: Stir very fast until a mixture is smooth. You can do this with a spoon, a whisk, or an electric or hand mixer.

Boil: Cook in water that has reached 212°F (boiling temperature).

Broil: Cook on a rack in the oven under direct heat.

Brown: Cook over high heat on the stove top to add darker color to food.

Chop: Cut food into small pieces, about the thickness of a pencil. If your recipe says "finely chopped," cut pieces to half that thickness.

Cream: Beat ingredients together until smooth.

Cube: Cut food into square pieces, typically about ½-inch wide.

Dash: A small amount, about ⅛ teaspoon.

Dice: Cut food into very small cubes, about ⅛-inch wide. Sometimes "dice" and "chop" are used interchangeably, but generally "dice" means smaller pieces than "chop."

Dust: Lightly cover (with powdered sugar, for instance), or lightly coat a surface or dough with flour.

Fold: Gently use a spatula to mix light ingredients (such as beaten egg whites) into heavier ingredients. The point of folding is to keep as much air in the mixture as possible.

Glaze: Coat food in sauce, icing, or other glossy liquids.

Grate: Rub food against a serrated grating tool to produce shredded bits.

Knead: Work dough ingredients together, using either your hands or an electric or hand mixer.

Mince: Cut ingredients into teeny-tiny pieces.

Pinch: A very small amount, about $\frac{1}{16}$ teaspoon.

Roast: Cook in dry heat in the oven.

Sauté: Cook over high heat on the stove top in a small amount of oil; also called "pan fry."

Shred: Cut into narrow strips using a knife or a grater.

Simmer: Heat liquid to just below the boiling point. You'll see bubbles forming on the surface but not yet bursting.

Slice: Cut into thin pieces.

To taste: Season a dish, usually with salt and pepper, until it tastes right to you—not too salty and not too bland!

Whip: Incorporate air into a mixture by using a whisk or a mixer.

Whisk: Incorporate air into a mixture or combine dry ingredients until smooth, using a fork or a whisk.

Zest: The outer part of a citrus fruit peel, or scraping or grating that peel.

Breakfasts

SERVES
4

PREP TIME
10 minutes

COOK TIME
30 minutes

3 tablespoons unsalted butter

1½ cups all-purpose flour

3½ teaspoons baking powder

1 tablespoon
granulated sugar

¼ teaspoon salt

1 large egg

1¼ cups whole milk

vegetable oil, for
greasing pan

Blueberry Syrup, for
serving (page 16)

Aralia Berry Jam and Pancakes

You don't need all the aralia juice in Salem to make the delicious jam in this recipe, but you will need a good handful of berries to squeeze. These pancakes will give you a nice little power-up in the morning— and, as we know, the aralia berry is a critical component in any truly powerful potion.

After a long night of dancing at town hall, escaping from 300-year-old (or 329-year-old) witches, or just hanging around in a cage over a giant cauldron, you'll need a hearty breakfast and a long nap. Start with these pancakes, adding the smoothie on page 17 if your evening was especially dire and stressful.

1. Over low heat, melt the butter in a small saucepan. Remove from the heat.

2. Sift the flour into a large bowl, then add the baking powder, sugar, and salt. Use a spoon to make a well in the center of the powder mixture.

3. Crack the egg into a small bowl and beat with a fork or wire whisk. Pour the beaten egg, melted butter, and milk into the well in the flour mixture. Mix with a wooden spoon until the batter is smooth and blended.

4. Heat a medium skillet on the stove top over medium heat. Grease with vegetable oil when warm, and then scoop ⅓ cup of the batter into the skillet. Cook until the pancake has browned on the bottom, then flip and continue cooking until both sides are browned. Serve immediately, or transfer pancakes to a baking sheet and keep them warm in the oven.

5. Continue the process until all the batter has been used. Between pancakes, wipe the skillet with a paper towel and regrease as needed to prevent the pancakes from burning.

6. Serve the pancakes warm along with the Blueberry Syrup.

2 cups frozen blueberries

1 cup granulated sugar

1 cup water

1 tablespoon lemon juice

Blueberry Syrup

1. Add the blueberries, sugar, and water to a small saucepan. Gently press some of the blueberries with a spoon to break the skins.

2. Turn on the burner heat to low, set the saucepan on the burner, and whisk the ingredients until the sugar dissolves, around 5 minutes.

3. Turn the heat up to medium and bring the berry mixture to a gentle boil, stirring continuously. Continue to stir often until the syrup thickens, about 5 minutes.

4. Remove from the heat and whisk in the lemon juice. Pour into a pitcher to serve.

Glorious Peanut Butter Smoothie

SERVES
2

PREP TIME
2 hours

COOK TIME
5 minutes

2 ripe bananas

½ cup peanut butter

2 cups whole milk

2 ice cubes

ground cinnamon or
unsweetened cocoa powder

Another glorious morning got you down? It's hard when you don't wake up younger in the morning. But don't get sick! Get yourself a delicious breakfast treat, like this protein-packed smoothie. Grown witches and witchlings alike will enjoy this heavenly smoothie featuring the sinfully delicious partnership of chocolate and peanut butter. In my opinion, the only combination that's better is a witch and her trusted booooooooook.

1. Cut up the bananas into slices and place in the freezer for at least 2 hours.
2. Add the cut bananas, peanut butter, milk, and ice cubes to a blender and blend at medium or high speed until smooth.
3. Pour into 2 glasses and add a dash of cinnamon or cocoa powder to each. Serve cold.

SERVES
10

PREP TIME
15 minutes

COOK TIME
20 minutes

12 large eggs

splash of water

sea salt, to taste

freshly cracked black
pepper, to taste

4 ounces grated
cheddar cheese

1 tablespoon unsalted butter

½ medium red
onion, chopped

1 cup chopped bell pepper

1 cup cherry tomatoes,
quartered

sliced green onions, for
garnish (optional)

Veggie Egg Cups

It was tough to be a kid in the '90s. You never knew if a day would bring bullies, romantic rejection, required chaperoning of your kid sister, or—you know—three ancient hags trying to suck out your life force. I'm sure it's no easier now, what with jocks who just don't get it, friends who trade up for love, and—you know—three ancient hags trying to suck out your life force.

No matter the era, experts all agree that the best way to get through it all is by having a strong sense of self, a positive attitude, and a good healthy breakfast. These frittata egg cups check that last box, and when kids take the lead in making them it can help develop confidence and a sense of self. Win-win! Now if only they could do something about those ancient hags.

1. Preheat the oven to 350°F.
2. Crack the eggs and add them to a large bowl along with a small splash of water and the sea salt and cracked black pepper. Whisk until the eggs are well beaten.
3. Add the cheese, mixing until evenly distributed.
4. Pour the egg-and-cheese mixture into a greased muffin tin so that 10 muffin cups are half filled.
5. Melt the butter in a skillet over medium heat. Add the chopped onion and sauté until soft and cooked through, or about 3 minutes.
6. Add the bell pepper and sauté for another 2 minutes. Transfer the vegetables to a large bowl.
7. Add the raw tomatoes and toss until the ingredients are evenly distributed.
8. Distribute the vegetable mixture into the egg-filled muffin tins.
9. Bake for 15 to 20 minutes, until the eggs are cooked and lightly browned. Remove from the oven and let cool for 3 to 5 minutes. Serve sprinkled with green onions, if using.

A Little Child's French Toast

SERVES
3

PREP TIME
5 minutes

COOK TIME
10 minutes

4 large eggs

dash of water

½ teaspoon vanilla extract

1 teaspoon ground cinnamon

½ tablespoon unsalted butter

6 slices white or whole grain bread

berries and whipped cream, for garnish

I always thought I'd have a child, and then I had one...on TOAST! A similar not-exactly-maternal comment uttered by our leading lady witch is easily missed if you're not attuned to the grisly humor of child-snack references. Lucky for you, I am.

If you prefer your toast childless, this French toast recipe can be made solo, but it is also perfectly easy to make with the help of one or two little children.

1. Crack the eggs into a wide bowl, such as a cereal bowl, and beat with a fork or wire whisk.

2. Add a dash of water, the vanilla extract, and the cinnamon; mix well.

3. Melt the butter in a medium frying pan over medium heat.

4. Soak the slices of bread one at a time in the beaten egg mixture and then fry in the butter. Flip to brown both sides. The French toast is done when it is browned on both sides and cooked in the middle. Serve immediately or transfer to a baking dish to keep warm in the oven.

5. Garnish with berries and whipped cream to serve.

SERVES
6

PREP TIME
10 minutes

COOK TIME
25 minutes

3 large eggs

½ cup whole milk

½ cup all-purpose flour

½ teaspoon sea salt, plus
more for sprinkling on top

4 ounces grated
gruyère cheese

3 tablespoons unsalted butter

Enchanting Cheese Gougère

A witch is nothing without thy coven, and a chef is nothing without a deceptively easy go-to brunch recipe. This skillet gougère is mostly egg and cheese, but I guarantee it will put a spell on kids and adults alike—trust me. I'm a witch. I know things.

As a quick personal aside, this is an incredibly easy recipe for a budding chef to help with. It was the very first thing my coven concocted together when my daughter started "helping" in the kitchen at 18 months. If you premeasure the cheese and flour into plastic bowls, even the littlest kitchen witch can help pour the ingredients and gently mix them together.

1. Preheat the oven to 400°F.
2. Beat the eggs in a large bowl using a fork or wire whisk.
3. Add the milk, flour, and sea salt to the eggs. Mix until all the ingredients are blended.
4. Use a spatula to gently fold in the grated cheese.
5. Melt the butter in a 9-inch cast-iron skillet. Use a spatula to coat the sides of the skillet with the butter.
6. Add the egg and cheese mixture to the skillet and sprinkle sea salt on top.
7. Bake until the eggs are cooked through and starting to brown, about 20 minutes. Remove from the oven, and cut into wedges. Serve warm.

SERVES
4

PREP TIME
5 minutes

COOK TIME
2 minutes

8 tablespoons milk
red, green, purple, and
orange food coloring
sliced white bread
butter
ground cinnamon

"Good Zombie" Toast

This toast was a huge hit with me and my siblings as kids in the '90s, and I think it stands the test of time. We called it monster toast, but it's a perfect way to pay homage to one good zombie!

What exactly qualifies as a good zombie? Well, if you're rudely awoken by the same person who killed you and tasked you with chasing almost-innocent children but you bravely refused, then you peacefully chill for 30 more years underground and still refuse to resort to zombie tropes—well, you definitely deserve the moniker "good zombie," along with a delicious and fun breakfast tribute!

Kids will love this recipe, as it is simple, allows for a bit of artistic creativity, and is just as much fun to eat as it is to prepare!

1. Pour 2 tablespoons of milk into each of 4 small bowls.
2. Pour 3 drops of each food coloring into its own bowl of milk. Add more food coloring to reach your desired colors. Stir gently until the color is mixed through.
3. Use a small arts or watercolor paintbrush to paint a pattern or picture on one side of the sliced white bread with the colored milks.
4. Toast the painted bread in a toaster or toaster oven. Then butter the toast and sprinkle with cinnamon and sugar, or any other desired topping, and serve warm.

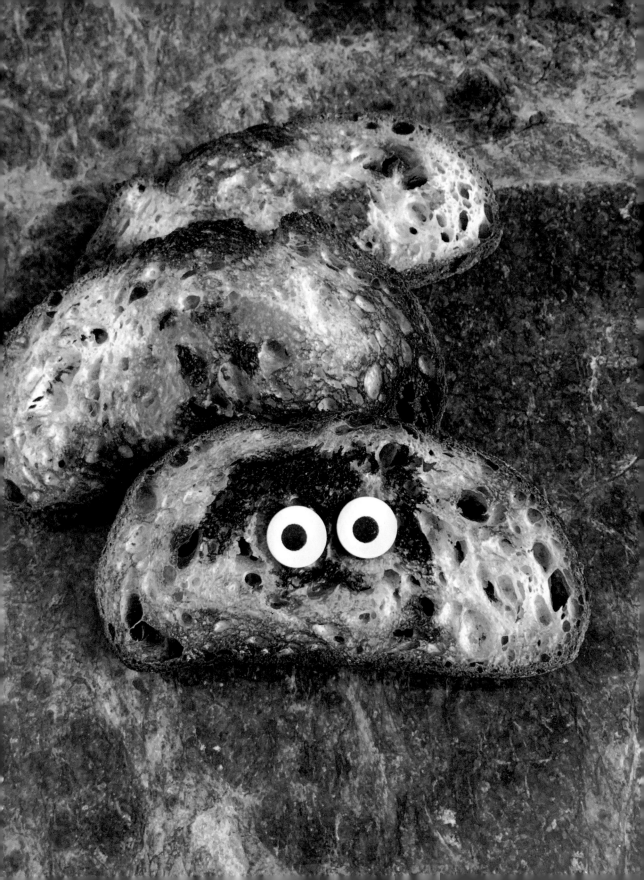

SERVES
4

PREP TIME
5 minutes

COOK TIME
5 minutes

1 banana

2 peaches

1 pear

2 cups almond milk

14 ounces frozen fruit mix
(such as mango, pineapple,
strawberry, and blueberry)

2 ounces (about 2 cups)
fresh spinach or kale

Tubular Smoothie

You don't have to live in L.A. to be "health conscious," and this kid-friendly smoothie makes it easy. Packed with fruits and vegetables, it makes a perfect after-school snack or energy-boosting breakfast. After all, it's tough to be a kid, particularly if you're being targeted by two brainless bullies and/or three ancient hags. The dose of vitamins in this smoothie will help keep wits sharp and feet fast.

1. Slice the banana (easy to do using a child-safe knife) and place in a blender.

2. Peel and slice the peaches and pear, discarding the seeds and core. Place in the blender along with the sliced banana.

3. Add the rest of the ingredients and blend well on medium to high speed.

4. Pour the blended smoothie into 4 glasses, or pour yourself a single serving now and divide the remainder into 8-ounce mason jars, filling each jar about three-fourths full. Seal the jars and place in the freezer to enjoy later. When you're ready for the next one, just thaw it in warm water or in the refrigerator to your desired consistency.

Mains

SERVES
6

PREP TIME
1½ hours

COOK TIME
20 minutes

4 cups flour
(use bread flour for a
crispier crust or all-purpose
flour for a doughier crust),
or more as needed.

1 teaspoon sugar

1 packet instant dry yeast

2 teaspoons salt

1½ cups warm water,
or more as needed

2½ tablespoons
olive oil, divided

1 small eggplant

1 green zucchini (or
one red onion)

1 pint cherry tomatoes

½ (28-ounce) can
crushed tomatoes

1 teaspoon garlic powder

1 teaspoon Italian seasoning

1 pound shredded
mozzarella cheese

Harvest Festival Pizza

Pizza is a perfect food for young witches to start helping with in the kitchen—there's limited cutting, the ingredients are easy, and everyone can pick their own toppings. For some added vitamins and autumnal flair, try this harvest vegetable pizza with seasonal squash, onion, broccoli, or even sweet potato. Even a little one who doesn't normally love vegetables will "lose their head" over the "cheese and crust!"

1. Attach the dough hook to a stand mixer. Pour the flour, sugar, yeast, and salt into the mixer bowl. Turn the mixer on medium speed to combine the ingredients.

2. While the mixer is combining the dry ingredients, add 1½ cups water and 2 tablespoons of the olive oil.

3. Mix until the dough forms into a solid ball. Use your hands to assess the consistency of the dough. For dough that is too dry, add water 1 tablespoon at a time while mixing. For dough that is too sticky, add flour 1 tablespoon at a time while mixing.

4. Remove the dough onto a floured surface and gently knead, then form into a smooth, firm ball.

5. Use the remaining ½ tablespoon olive oil to grease the inside of a large bowl. Transfer the dough to the bowl and cover with plastic wrap. Let the dough sit in a warm area for about 1 hour, until it expands to twice its original size.

6. Remove the dough to a lightly floured surface and divide it into 2 equal-size pieces. Cover each piece with plastic wrap and let it sit for an additional 10 minutes.

7. Set the rack low in the oven and preheat the oven to 400°F. If you will be using a pizza stone, insert it in the oven now.

8. Chop the eggplant, zucchini, and cherry tomatoes to the shapes and sizes you want for your pizza toppings.

9. Unwrap a dough ball of dough and stretch and pound it into the shape and size you want. Place it on a rimmed baking sheet or stone.

10. Pour the crushed tomatoes over the dough and spread evenly with a spoon or spatula.

11. Sprinkle on the garlic powder and Italian seasoning.

12. Sprinkle the cheese over the surface of the pizza.

13. Distribute the vegetables over the pizza surface. Repeat steps 9 to 13 for the second ball of dough, or you can freeze the extra dough for up to 3 months.

14. Place one pizza in the oven on the pan or stone and bake until the cheese is bubbling and the pizza is lightly browned on the bottom, about 20 minutes.

15. Remove the pizza from the oven and let cool for 5 minutes. Then transfer to a board to cut and serve.

SERVES
4

PREP TIME
20 minutes

COOK TIME
20 minutes

2 large boneless, skinless
chicken breasts

1 bell pepper, any color

1 white onion

2 cloves garlic

1 tablespoon unsalted butter

½ taco seasoning packet

1 tablespoon olive oil

2 cups shredded sharp
cheddar cheese

4 large flour tortillas

½ cup sour cream, for dipping

Full Moon Quesadilla

Feeling the icy breath of death—I mean dinnertime—upon your neck? Here's a quick, easy, and delicious supper recipe for a coven that's getting hangry.

1. Cut the chicken breasts into bite-size pieces.
2. Dice the bell pepper and cut the onion into quarters (these tasks are easily done using a child-safe knife).
3. Finely chop the garlic cloves.
4. Melt the butter in a large skillet over medium-high heat. When the butter is hot and glistening, add the chicken pieces. Sauté the chicken until it starts to brown and then add the taco seasoning and onion quarters. Stir to combine.
5. Let the chicken and onion cook for 2 to 3 minutes and then add the garlic and diced bell pepper. Continue cooking for about 5 minutes, until the chicken and vegetables are cooked through, stirring occasionally.
6. Add the olive oil to another skillet over medium heat. Place a tortilla in the skillet and top with some of the cheese and the chicken and vegetable filling. Top with more cheese.
7. Using a spatula, carefully fold the filled tortilla in half (an older witch may be able to help with this step). Flip the tortilla so that it browns on both sides. Serve immediately, or transfer to a baking sheet to keep warm in the oven. Repeat until you run out of tortillas and filling.
8. Cut each quesadilla into 4 triangular pieces and serve with the sour cream for dipping. (For a young child, serving in large, finger-shaped slices may be preferable.)

> **TIP:** If you buy a block of cheese and grate it yourself, it will generally melt faster and more uniformly than pre-shredded cheese.

Oil of Boil Soup

SERVES
10

PREP TIME
15 minutes

COOK TIME
50 minutes

2 boneless, skinless chicken breasts

salt, pepper, and garlic powder, to taste

1 white onion

4 cloves garlic

3 tablespoons olive oil

1 cup diced carrots

1 cup diced celery

8 cups chicken stock

8 ounces orzo pasta

1 (14-ounce) can diced tomatoes

½ teaspoon dried thyme

½ teaspoon oregano

¼ teaspoon dried rosemary

4 to 5 ounces (4 cups, packed) fresh spinach

There's no need to add a bit of thine own tongue to this potion. Your tongue will thank thee, no doubt, for leaving it intact, and again for tasting this positively divine soup. A simple, easy, and delicious soup recipe can be as difficult to find as a talking cat, but this one fits the bill and is sure to be a whole-family pleaser for at least 300 years to come.

1. Preheat the oven to 350°F.

2. Season the chicken breasts with salt, pepper, and garlic powder. Bake on a baking sheet in the oven for 25 to 30 minutes, until cooked through.

3. While the chicken is baking, dice the white onion. Cut the garlic cloves into thin slices.

4. When the chicken is cooked, remove it from the oven and let it cool slightly. Shred it or cut it into bite-size chunks.

5. Heat the olive oil in a large stockpot or Dutch oven over medium heat. Add the onion and sauté until it is soft and fragrant, about 3 minutes. Add the carrots, celery, and garlic and sauté for an additional 3 minutes.

6. Add the chicken stock, orzo, chicken pieces, tomatoes, thyme, oregano, and rosemary. Stir to combine.

7. Bring the soup to a simmer, then reduce the heat slightly and let simmer for 10 minutes, stirring occasionally.

8. When the orzo is cooked to the texture you want, add the spinach and cook for an additional 2 minutes.

9. Season with salt and pepper and serve warm.

SERVES
4

PREP TIME
15 minutes

COOK TIME
35 minutes

1 large red onion

4 cloves garlic

1 large sweet potato

2 tablespoons olive oil

pinch of salt

1 ½ tablespoons chili powder

2 teaspoons ground cumin

1 teaspoon dried oregano

½ teaspoon ground
cayenne pepper

1 teaspoon paprika

1 (14.5-ounce) can fire-
roasted diced tomatoes

2 ½ teaspoons unsweetened
cocoa powder

2 cups vegetable broth

⅔ cup frozen corn

1 ½ teaspoons sea salt

freshly cracked
pepper, to taste

1 ½ (15-ounce) cans black
beans, drained and rinsed

2 tablespoons freshly
squeezed lime juice

vegan tortilla chips,
for garnish

sliced avocado, for garnish

Listing Vegan Foods Chili

Tempeh, soyrizo, aquafaba garbanzo...okay, while I am literally listing vegan foods, none of these actually makes an appearance in this chili. Some of them do sound a bit otherworldly, though, so it is easy to imagine them listed in an ancient spellbook.

The ingredients in this vegan chili are much more straightforward. If you have any vegans in your coven, this is sure to be a hit. If you don't, just don't tell them that it's vegan, and they'll never have to know!

1. Dice the red onion. Mince the garlic cloves. Peel the sweet potato and cut into ½-inch chunks.

2. In a Dutch oven, heat the olive oil over medium heat. When the oil is hot and shimmering, add the diced onion and a pinch of salt. Sauté until the onion pieces are translucent and cooked through, about 3 minutes.

3. Add the garlic and sauté for another minute, stirring gently so that it doesn't burn.

4. Add the sweet potato pieces, chili powder, cumin, oregano, and cayenne. Sauté for about a minute and then add the canned tomatoes and cocoa powder; stir until well blended.

5. Add the broth, corn, sea salt, and pepper, mixing well. Partially cover the Dutch oven with its lid and bring the chili to a simmer, then reduce the heat slightly so that the mixture continues to simmer without reaching a rolling boil. Simmer for 15 minutes, partially covered, occasionally stirring to prevent the ingredients from burning and sticking to the bottom.

6. Add the beans, stirring to blend them into the chili. Let the chili simmer, partially covered, for another 10 minutes so the broth cooks down and thickens slightly. Test to see if the chili is ready by stabbing sweet potato pieces with a fork to ensure they are soft and cooked through.

7. Remove the chili from the heat and stir in the lime juice.

8. Serve in bowls, garnished with tortilla chips and sliced avocado.

Twist Thy (Chicken) Fingers

SERVES
4

PREP TIME
20 minutes

COOK TIME
20 minutes

2 pounds boneless, skinless chicken breast

3 large eggs

dash of water

2 cups whole wheat flour

2 cups seasoned panko bread crumbs

¼ cup grated parmesan cheese

1 tablespoon garlic powder

salt and pepper, to taste

½ cup olive oil

1 head romaine lettuce

1 pint cherry tomatoes

dressing of choice

Plump juicy hen, long since dead,

Laid across a soft green bed,

Dipped and breaded, battered and fried,

Served with tomatoes on the side.

Kids will love a filet or thigh,

And gobble it up, so say I!

1. Preheat the oven to 375°F.
2. Cut the chicken breasts into chicken finger–sized strips.
3. Crack the eggs into a large bowl. Add a dash of water and whisk well with a fork or wire whisk.
4. Pour the flour onto a large plate.
5. On a separate large plate, combine the bread crumbs, cheese, garlic powder, salt, and pepper, mixing well.
6. Pat the chicken strips dry using a paper towel. Then dip each piece into the flour to coat all sides. Shake off any excess flour.
7. Dip each floured chicken piece in the whipped eggs, then coat in the bread crumb mixture.
8. Drizzle about half of the olive oil onto a rimmed cookie sheet and arrange the chicken pieces on the oil. Drizzle the remaining olive oil on the chicken.
9. Transfer the pan to the oven and bake for about 10 minutes, then flip the chicken pieces over. Bake for an additional 10 minutes, or until well browned.
10. While the chicken is baking, chop the lettuce and tomatoes. Toss with your favorite dressing and divide between the 4 plates.
11. Remove the chicken from the oven and serve over the bed of lettuce and tomatoes.

SERVES
4

PREP TIME
30 minutes

COOK TIME
6 minutes

1 tablespoon fresh parsley, chopped

6 sprigs fresh rosemary

6 sprigs fresh thyme

6 leaves fresh sage

4 cloves garlic

½ teaspoon sea salt

½ teaspoon crushed black pepper

12 lamb rib chops

3 tablespoon extra-virgin olive oil

Dead Man's Chungs Lamb Rib Chops

It was nearly 30 years ago that the world first learned about the existence of chungs. What are they, exactly? Do all men have them or just deceased ones? Is it possible for all people to possess chungs?

Now that the world's favorite witches have died for the third (but is it the final?) time, we may never learn the answers to these questions, and we may have forever lost the magickal knowledge and ingredients to make a well-brewed Life Potion. Perhaps this is for the best. The world certainly doesn't need any more witches trying to snatch the lives of children, but it could use a recipe for perfectly moist and easy grilled rib chops.

1. Finely chop the fresh herbs and garlic, setting aside enough chopped parsley to use as garnish. Mix together the rest of the herbs and garlic in a small bowl with the sea salt and black pepper.

2. Place the chops on a baking sheet and brush the lamb chops with the olive oil, coating them well.

3. Coat the lamb chops with the herb and spice blend, then let them sit for 20 minutes to reach room temperature. Meanwhile, turn the grill on high so the temperature reaches at least 500°F.

4. Grill the lamb chops over high heat for 3 minutes and then flip them over. This should give them a charred exterior and a medium rare interior. (You can grill them longer if you prefer a more well-done chop.)

5. Transfer to a serving plate, sprinkle with parsley, and serve immediately.

SERVES
8

PREP TIME
25 minutes

COOK TIME
20 minutes

2 large eggs

2 pounds ground chuck

1 ½ cups Italian seasoned bread crumbs

½ cup chopped parsley

½ teaspoon garlic powder

1 teaspoon dried oregano

¼ cup water, or more as needed

1 cup grated parmesan cheese

¼ cup olive oil

Black Magic Meatballs

All Hallow's Eve may have become a night of frolic, but dinner should be serious—or at least hearty—before you and/or your coven begin running amok. These meatballs are the perfect choice. Serve them with tomato sauce or fried with fresh veggies and they'll be exactly what any cool teenager needs to fuel a long night of shenanigans.

1. Preheat the oven to 350°F.
2. Crack the 2 eggs into a small bowl. Beat well using a fork or wire whisk.
3. Transfer the eggs to a large bowl and add all the other ingredients except the olive oil. Roll up your sleeves and mix with your hands until everything is well blended. Make sure to break up any cheese chunks.
4. As you mix, you may decide to add an additional ¼ cup of water to make sure the mixture is moist.
5. Grease 2 baking sheets or spray with nonstick spray.
6. Roll the meat mixture into evenly sized balls. (I prefer meatballs slightly bigger than a golf ball.). Arrange on the cookie sheets with about 1 inch of space between them.
7. Use a pastry brush to brush the tops of the meatballs with olive oil.
8. Bake for about 20 minutes, or until the meatballs are browned on the outside and very slightly crisped on the bottom.
9. Remove from the pans quickly and transfer to a serving dish.

VARIATION: To add more nutrition for a little one, replace half the beef chuck with ground turkey. Then puree some cooked carrots and raw spinach in a blender and add about ½ cup of the puree to the meatball mixture before you add the ¼ cup water. The puree will add moisture, so you may decide to reduce the amount of water to keep the meatballs from being too soft.

SERVES
6

PREP TIME
15 minutes

COOK TIME
90 minutes

¼ cup fresh rosemary

¾ cup fresh thyme

½ cup fresh oregano

3 medium lemons

3 tablespoons dehydrated garlic flakes

1 tablespoon sea salt

olive oil

3-pound rump roast

Angelica Leaves Herb Blend and Aged Roast

Burning these herbs won't lift a curse, but using this blend will ward off the hex of a flavorless roast. Normally you'd want your meal to be as young—I mean fresh—as possible, but in this case a perfectly aged piece of beef will have more flavor and be as tender as an innocent young child.

1. Preheat the oven to its lowest temperature.
2. Remove the stems from the fresh rosemary, thyme, and oregano. Finely chop the herbs and mix together in a small bowl.
3. Zest the lemons, then spread the lemon zest and herbs across a rimmed cookie sheet lined with parchment paper.
4. Place the cookie sheet in the middle of the oven and bake for 2 to 4 hours, tossing the mixture every 30 minutes.
5. When the herbs and lemon zest feel dry, remove the cookie sheet from the oven and set it aside to cool.
6. When cool, combine the herbs and lemon zest in a small bowl with the garlic flakes and sea salt.
7. Preheat the oven to 325°F.
8. Rub the roast with the olive oil to coat well, then rub with the herb blend.
9. Set the roast on a rack in a roasting pan. Place in the middle of the oven and cook for about 1½ hours. Remove the roast from the oven when the internal temperature reaches 135°F for medium rare or 145°F for medium.
10. Tent the roast with aluminum foil and let sit for 10 minutes to let the internal temperature rise to 145°F for medium rare or 155°F for medium.
11. Cut in thin slices to serve.

SERVES
8

PREP TIME
15 minutes

COOK TIME
20 minutes

8 hot dogs
1 package Pillsbury
crescent rolls

Homemade Mustard
½ cup dry ground
yellow mustard
½ cup water
⅓ cup apple cider vinegar
1 teaspoon all-purpose flour
¾ teaspoon salt
¼ teaspoon ground turmeric
⅛ teaspoon garlic powder
⅛ teaspoon smoked paprika

Dead Man's Toes

Unlike newt saliva, oil of boil, or a bit of thine own tongue, a dead man's toe (especially a fresh one) is not the easiest of potion ingredients to come by. At least it wasn't in the 1600s.

When you don't have access to a life potion with young souls already mixed in, the dead man's toe is a critical component. But now, with modern technology, it's easy to have access to as many dead man's toes as you need, whether it's for a whole party or just a little solo potion-brewing.

1. Preheat the oven to 375°F. Grease a cookie sheet or coat with nonstick spray.
2. Cut each hot dog in half crosswise to make 2 short hot dogs.
3. Open the crescent roll container and unroll the dough. Cut into 16 similar-size triangles.
4. Roll each hot dog half with a crescent roll triangle so that the cut half of the hot dog is wrapped in the dough and the uncut half is sticking out.
5. Using a sharp paring knife, make 2 or 3 thin, shallow slits on the top side of each hot dog right at the edge of the crescent roll dough (this will be the knuckle).
6. Cut a long half-oval out of the top of the hot dog at the uncut end, to look like a fingernail bed.
7. Place the hot dogs on the greased cookie sheet, cut side up, and bake for approximately 12 minutes.
8. While the hot dogs are baking, make the Homemade Mustard. Combine the mustard, water, vinegar, flour, salt, turmeric, garlic powder, and paprika in a small saucepan over medium heat. Whisk well as you bring the mixture to a boil. Let the mixture boil for 8 minutes, stirring to keep it from burning. Then remove from the stove top and let cool for 5 minutes.
9. Remove the hot dogs from the oven and use the mustard to "paint" the toenails of the hot dogs. Serve with extra mustard for dipping.
10. Transfer any unused mustard to a jar, seal, and store in the refrigerator.

Halloween Party Snack Board

SERVES
4

PREP TIME
20 minutes

COOK TIME
0 minutes

4 ounces of your favorite cheese, cut into thin slices

1 small celery stalk, cut into pieces about ½ inch wide and 1 inch long

4 mandarin oranges, peeled

2 ounces prosciutto or other cured meat

½ cup pimiento-stuffed green olives

1 cup candy-coated chocolates, or other small candy of your choice

½ cup chocolate-coated caramels, or other small candy of your choice

1 cup Skittles

½ cup gummy worms

2 to 4 Krispy Rice Boooooooks (page 105) or Black Flame Candle Pretzels (page 106), optional

1 cup pretzel crisps

1 cup bagel chips or other cracker

The "old days" of Lunchables might be dead but millennial witches can get their fix with this elevated snack board, perfect for bringing to a Halloween party—whether it's your ex–best friend's, down at the town hall, or hosted by rich people.

Even the smallest witches in training can take the lead on this recipe, since it relies mostly on prepared foods—you know, ones with the souls already mixed in. This is the perfect opportunity to practice creativity in the kitchen. If you don't have an ingredient in your potions larder, see what you can substitute from what you do have (it's easy to swap out the candies, in particular—just NO licorice). Potions and spells might require intricate instructions and complicated chants, but kitchen magic is all about riffing—experimenting and honing your skills!

1. Arrange the cheese slices in the middle of a platter—in a line, a pile, whatever shape suits you.

2. Insert a celery strip into the top of each peeled mandarin orange so they look like pumpkins. Arrange on the platter. (I like to group a couple of them together and then separate the others so it's not too symmetrical.)

3. Arrange the prosciutto or other meat in a small pile next to the cheese.

4. Put the olives in a small bowl across from the pair of pumpkins, or wherever you like on the platter.

5. Place 1 or 2 Krispy Rice Boooooooks toward the middle of the platter.

6. Arrange a couple of Black Flame Candle Pretzels on the platter with the flames pointing outward. Fill in the open spaces with pretzel crisps and bagel chips.

SERVES
6

PREP TIME
15 minutes

COOK TIME
6 hours 15 minutes

3 pounds corned beef brisket, flat cut, with spice packet

2 tablespoons light brown sugar

5 cloves garlic

1½ cups beef broth

2 tablespoons butter, divided

2 ¼-inch slices white onion, cut into half-moon shapes

1 teaspoon granulated sugar

1 tablespoon homemade mustard (page 46)

2 teaspoons Worcestershire sauce

2 slices sourdough or rye bread

4 slices Jarlsberg cheese

Trapped in Salt Corned Beef Grilled Cheese

Salt is the workhorse of both the kitchen and black magic defense. When used appropriately it can transform a slab of beef into a juicy and tender meal, or a standard suburban garage into a trap for a gaggle of gothic golden girls. If you're a witch, getting trapped in salt is likely your doom, but if you're a delicious brisket, it is your savior. These easy grilled sandwiches use salt-brined beef brisket and a savory homemade mustard that will delight anyone from children to withering hags (zombie's words, not mine!).

1. Season the corned beef with the seasoning packet and place in a slow cooker, fat side up.

2. Add the brown sugar, garlic, and beef broth to the Crockpot. Cook on low for 6 hours. The corned beef is ready when the inside temperature reaches 145˚F and the meat is tender.

3. When the corned beef is done cooking, transfer it onto a cutting board and let it rest for 15 minutes. Then cut the corned beef into ½-inch slices.

4. Melt 1 tablespoon butter in a skillet over medium heat. Add the onion slices and sugar and sauté until the onions are see-through.

5. Add enough sliced corned beef for one sandwich, along with the Worcestershire sauce. Turn off the heat and mix the contents until well blended.

6. Butter one side of the sourdough bread slices. Place 2 slices of Jarlsberg cheese on the unbuttered side of each slice. Place a slice of bread, buttered side down, in the skillet. Scoop the corned beef mixture on top of the cheese and then top with 2 more slices of cheese and the second slice of bread.

7. Turn the burner back on to medium heat and cook the sandwich until the bread is brown, then flip it to brown the second side. Slice in half and serve warm. Repeat steps 5 to 8 for the rest of the corned beef (about 5 more sandwiches) or store the corned beef in an airtight container in the refrigerator for up to 5 days.

SERVES
5

PREP TIME
25 minutes

COOK TIME
0 minutes

3 Brie rounds, about
5 to 6 inches wide

½ pound cased pepperoni
cut into ½ inch cubes

½ pound white cheddar
cheese, cubed

1 pint (2 cups) blackberries

3 pitted black olives

5 or 6 strawberries

assorted crackers

Fresh-Faced Cheese Platter

There's a power greater than magic, and that's knowing how to put together a gorgeous snack platter! If you can artfully arrange food on a plate, platter, or board, you won't need an enchanting singing voice to lure people to your home.

Yes, this is the second snack platter recipe in this book, but like the souls of young children, you can never have too many snack platters. The key to this one is the witches' likenesses. Feel free to fill out the rest of the board as you wish (or combine with the snack board on page 49).

1. Place the Brie rounds on a platter. You can scatter them or line them up.

2. Arrange the cubes of pepperoni above one of the Brie rounds to make 2 adjoining triangles.

3. Place the cheddar cheese cubes above the second Brie round. Arrange them up and over to one side—like hair cascading over a witch's shoulder.

4. Pile the blackberries above the last Brie round, in a cone shape that tilts to one side.

5. Slice the olives into slivers, then place 2 slivers on each Brie round as eyes.

6. Cut slivers from a strawberry and position one on each Brie round as a mouth.

7. Arrange the rest of the berries and crackers around the board, filling in with whatever else you have in your pantry—pretzels, grapes, other fruits. You can also use the Eye Cream Cookie Dip on page 78 to pair with your fruits.

SERVES
4

PREP TIME
5 hours 20 minutes

COOK TIME
20 minutes

1 envelope taco seasoning

2 tablespoons olive oil

1 cup tomato juice

2 pounds raw chicken breast, cut into bite-size cubes

6 to 8 wooden skewers

1 green bell pepper

1 orange bell pepper

1 red onion

1 zucchini or squash

2 cups white button mushrooms

Shush Ke Baby Tacos

Every food is more fun when skewered on a stick—hot dogs, marshmallows, even children—I mean tacos. These deconstructed chicken taco skewers, cooked on a grill, are an easy dinner to whip up on a weeknight or anytime you need a fast Anti-Hunger Spell. Get the whole coven involved by having your witches choose and skewer their own ingredients in whatever order or pattern they like.

1. In a medium bowl, mix together the taco seasoning, olive oil, and tomato juice. Transfer ½ cup of the mixture to a separate small bowl; cover and refrigerate.

2. Add the chicken cubes to the remaining marinade blend and mix until they are well-coated. Then refrigerate, covered, for 5 hours.

3. Soak the wooden skewers in water for 30 minutes.

4. Cut the bell peppers, squash or zucchini, and onion into large bite-sized chunks.

5. Spear the chicken and vegetables with the wooden skewers, alternating chicken with vegetables as desired. Leave an inch and a half to two inches on each end to hold the skewer.

6. Grill uncovered over medium-high heat for about 3 minutes on each side. Then baste with the reserved ½ cup taco marinade and grill for approximately 8 to 10 more minutes, turning as needed to cook evenly.

7. Remove to a platter to serve.

> **NOTE:** If you have the time, whip up this luscious rémoulade sauce to drizzle over the Shush Ke Baby Tacos—it is marvelous. To make the sauce, in a medium bowl, add 4 finely chopped green onions, 1 minced garlic clove, 1 cup of mayonnaise, ¼ cup of chili sauce, 2 tablespoons of Creole mustard, 2 tablespoons of olive oil, 1 tablespoon of Louisiana-style chili pepper hot sauce, 2 tablespoons of fresh lemon juice, 1 teaspoon of Worcestershire sauce, 2 tablespoons of chopped parsley, ½ teaspoon of Cajun seasoning, 1 teaspoon of salt, ½ teaspoon of pepper, and 1 teaspoon of Old Bay seasoning. Blend well using a rubber spatula. Cover and refrigerate for at least 3 hours before using.

SERVES
6

PREP TIME
15 minutes

COOK TIME
4½ hours

4 cloves garlic

2 tablespoons olive oil

1 (28-ounce) can crushed San Marzano tomatoes

1 (28-ounce) can peeled San Marzano tomatoes

1 (6-ounce) can tomato paste

2 teaspoons dried basil

½ teaspoon oregano

½ white onion

1 pound ziti pasta

1 pound shredded mozzarella cheese

8 ounces ricotta cheese

Baked Witch Ziti

This is a crowd-pleasing pasta casserole, and an easy one at that—especially since you only need your standard kitchen stove and a slow cooker, not an industrial-grade kiln. Not only is this meal simple and delicious but it freezes well, too, so you can make a batch and resurrect it later (though I wouldn't store it for more than 6 months, much less 300 years). I promise that your coven will request this meal more often than a gaggle of witches can die.

1. Peel and thinly slice the garlic, then sauté it in the olive oil in a small skillet over medium heat until fragrant, or about 3 minutes.
2. Pour the cooked garlic and olive oil into a blender. Add the crushed and peeled tomatoes, tomato paste, basil, and oregano and blend on low speed until fully combined.
3. Pour the contents of the blender into a slow cooker. Add the onion half, cover, and cook on high heat until the mixture starts to bubble, approximately 30 minutes.
4. Reduce the heat to low and let the sauce simmer for 4 hours. When the sauce is ready, remove the half onion.
5. Fill a large pot with salted water. Bring to a boil on the stove top over high heat.
6. Preheat the oven to 350°F.
7. Add the pasta to the boiling water and cook according to the package directions.
8. Just before the pasta is fully cooked, scoop out about ⅓ cup of the pasta water and add it to the sauce.
9. Strain the pasta and transfer it to a large mixing bowl. Add about two-thirds of the tomato sauce, reserving the rest for topping the casserole. Add the ricotta and mozzarella cheeses, setting aside enough mozzarella to sprinkle on top. Blend well.
10. Pour the ziti into a large baking dish or large cast-iron skillet. Top with the reserved tomato sauce and mozzarella. Bake until the cheese is melted and the sauce is bubbling, about 20 minutes.
11. Remove the baked ziti from the oven and let sit for 10 minutes to set. Serve warm.

Sides

SERVES
8

PREP TIME
15 minutes

COOK TIME
1 hour 20 minutes

5 large russet potatoes, scrubbed and patted dry

½ pound bacon

¾ cup sour cream*

½ cup half-and-half*

6 tablespoons unsalted butter

¾ teaspoon salt

½ teaspoon pepper

1 cup grated sharp cheddar cheese

8 green onion leaves, chopped

*Or more, as needed to achieve the desired consistency.

Spell for Reuniting Potatoes

Have you ever wanted something very badly, only to get it and realize that what you really wanted was what you already had? Whether it's regretting asking for siblings or giving up your siblings and wishing you had them back, or just pleading for chicken nuggets only to realize that what you actually wanted was a quesadilla, this is a situation humans know all too well. Luckily, the solution is here, These twice-baked potatoes are a dish you will love no matter what you thought you wanted. Just make sure you're really ready for the consequences—because once you make this, you'll never be able to go back to a time when you didn't know just how buttery and delicious a humble potato could be.

1. Preheat the oven to 400°F.
2. Poke holes in each potato with a fork, longways along the center where you'll later cut the potato in half.
3. Place the potatoes on the oven rack and bake until tender, approximately 1 hour depending on their size. (Check for doneness by piercing with a fork.) Remove the potatoes from the oven and set aside until cool enough to handle.
4. While the potatoes are baking, fry the bacon in a skillet over medium-high heat. Chop the cooked bacon into small pieces.
5. Slice the baked potatoes in half lengthwise. Then scoop out the insides with a spoon, being careful not to pierce the skins.
6. Transfer the potato flesh to a bowl and, with a potato masher, mash together with the sour cream, half-and-half, butter, salt, and pepper. Add more half and half or sour cream if necessary to achieve the desired creaminess.
7. Set aside enough bacon, cheddar cheese, and green onions for garnishing. Fold the rest into the potatoes.
8. Turn the oven to 350°F. Fill 8 of the 10 potato halves with the mashed potatoes so they are overflowing. Top with bacon and cheddar cheese and bake until the cheese is melted, about 5 minutes. Discard the unused potato skins.
9. Remove from the oven, garnish with chopped green onions, and serve.

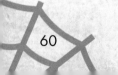

SERVES
4

PREP TIME
10 minutes

COOK TIME
45 minutes

1 large head cauliflower

3 cloves garlic

⅓ cup grated pecorino romano cheese

⅓ cup olive oil

1 teaspoon dried basil

1 teaspoon dried parsley

1 teaspoon dried thyme

½ teaspoon sea salt

¼ teaspoon crushed black pepper

Head of a Lover

While the head of a lover long since dead is a critical ingredient in a Power Spell, the head required for this recipe should ideally be a bit fresher, and locally sourced if possible—the magic and power of a place can have a profound effect on magic of all kinds. Why else do you think witches need to charge their magic in certain sacred spots and are forbidden from certain others?

This roasted head of cauliflower will give you all the power you need, and is simple, easy, and delicious to boot.

1. Preheat the oven to 400°F.
2. Using a sharp knife, remove the stem of the cauliflower head so the bottom is flat. Be careful not to cut too close to the head so that the cauliflower florets remain intact.
3. Chop the garlic into fine pieces.
4. Set aside 2 tablespoons of the grated cheese. In a medium bowl, combine the rest of the cheese with the olive oil, garlic, basil, parsley, thyme, sea salt, and black pepper. Stir until well combined.
5. Place the cauliflower head in a Dutch oven, stem side down. Drizzle the olive oil mixture over the cauliflower to coat the head and the stem. If necessary, use a pastry brush to evenly distribute the oil mixture.
6. Cover with the lid and bake for 40 minutes, or until the cauliflower is easily pierced with a fork.
7. Take the Dutch oven out of the oven and turn on the broiler. Remove the lid from the Dutch oven and sprinkle the head of the cauliflower with the reserved 2 tablespoons grated cheese.
8. Place the Dutch oven under the broiler, uncovered, for 5 minutes. Remove from the oven, cut into quarters and serve the cauliflower warm.

SERVES
8

PREP TIME
10 minutes

COOK TIME
20 minutes

½ cup (1 stick) unsalted butter

2¼ tablespoons vegetable oil, divided

2 cups self-rising cornmeal mix

2 medium eggs

1 to 1¾ cups buttermilk

⅓ cup honey

2 tablespoons vanilla extract

Corn, I Smell Cornbread

Any super smellers in your coven will be delighted to assist in making this recipe—probably happier with this than with a scrod dish, say.

Corn is a well-loved summer side, but warm skillet cornbread fresh from the oven can be a lovely autumnal choice—particularly when spread with fresh honey-vanilla butter.

1. Preheat the oven to 400°F and set the butter out to soften.
2. Pour ¼ tablespoon of the vegetable oil into a 9-inch cast-iron skillet and heat on the stove top over high heat.
3. While the oil is heating, combine the cornmeal, 2 tablespoons of vegetable oil, eggs, and 1 cup buttermilk in a large bowl and stir together with a spoon. Add more buttermilk if needed; the batter should be thick but pourable.
4. When the oil in the skillet is hot and simmering, pour in the batter. Transfer the skillet to the oven and bake for 25 to 30 minutes or until the edges are golden.
5. While the cornbread bakes, combine the softened butter, honey, and vanilla in a small bowl. Mix well with a fork or spoon.
6. Serve the cornbread warm with the honey-vanilla butter.

SERVES
6 to 8

PREP TIME
10 minutes

COOK TIME
1 hour

1 pound sweet potatoes

½ cup light brown sugar, packed

¼ teaspoon ground ginger

1 (15-ounce) can sliced peaches, well drained

3 tablespoons unsalted butter

Peach Sunrise Sweet Potato Casserole

This was a common recipe in my coven when I was but a little child. Some mothers make scorpion pie, but mine made peach sweet potato casserole every Thanksgiving. Sweet potatoes make a wonderful autumn side dish that can be dressed up or down—and that sticks to your ribs, giving you the complex carbs you need for a night of mischief, mayhem, or running for your life.

While typically thought of as a summer fruit, peaches are simply marvelous in this dish, and canned peach slices look just like the glowing rays of a sunrise that promises safety—or death, depending on whom you ask.

1. Peel the sweet potatoes and cut them into thick chunks.
2. In a large pot over high heat, boil the sweet potatoes in enough water to cover them. Boil until they are cooked but still firm when pierced with a fork, about 15 minutes.
3. Preheat the oven to 350°F.
4. Combine the brown sugar and ginger in a small bowl.
5. In a 10 x 6 x 2-inch baking dish, layer half the sweet potatoes, then half the peaches, and then half the brown sugar mixture. Repeat the layers.
6. Dot the top with the butter and cover with aluminum foil.
7. Bake, covered, for 30 minutes. Then remove the cover and bake for an additional 10 minutes.
8. When you serve, be sure to scoop up the extra brown sugar syrup that will have formed in the bottom of the pan, for extra deliciousness.

Newt Saliva and Fries

SERVES
6

PREP TIME
45 minutes

COOK TIME
20 minutes

¾ cup mayonnaise

3 cloves garlic, minced

1 ½ tablespoons lemon juice, or more if desired

¾ teaspoon sea salt, plus more for sprinkling

½ teaspoon paprika

⅓ teaspoon pepper

fresh parsley, chopped, for garnish

3 pounds russet potatoes

vegetable oil

Any witch—or budding chef—needs a basic understanding of potions and sauces. Newt saliva is a common ingredient in many standard potions, making it a versatile and important ingredient. Similarly, a basic aioli recipe is a versatile sauce to have in your repertoire. It can be dressed up and customized for any number of recipes.

Lemon and garlic give this aioli the perfect fresh taste to accompany a deliciously crunchy French fry.

1. In a small bowl, combine the mayonnaise, minced garlic, lemon juice, ¾ teaspoon sea salt, paprika, and pepper; mix well. (You can add more lemon juice or seasoning, if you wish.) Cover the aioli sauce and place in the refrigerator to chill.

2. Cut the potatoes into matchstick shapes, about a quarter inch thick. You can peel the potato skins or leave them on.

3. Soak the cut potatoes in a bowl of cold water for 30 minutes. Then drain and pat dry with paper towels.

4. In a large pot, heat approximately 3 inches of vegetable oil over medium heat. If you are using a thermometer, the oil should reach 300°F.

5. Fry the potatoes in the oil in batches, about 3 minutes per batch. (Kids doing this should have an adult's help.) Using a mesh sieve or a pair of tongs, transfer the fried potatoes to a cookie sheet lined with a paper towel to catch the excess oil.

6. Now turn the heat to high; the oil should reach 400°F.

7. Refry the potatoes in batches until they are golden brown, about 2 minutes per batch. Transfer onto the paper towel–lined cookie sheet.

8. Sprinkle with sea salt to taste. Garnish with parsley and serve with the aioli for dipping.

SERVES
6

PREP TIME
5 minutes

COOK TIME
20 minutes

1 (15-ounce) can chickpeas
1 tablespoon olive oil
1 tablespoon garlic powder
1 teaspoon sea salt
½ teaspoon pepper
½ teaspoon paprika

Petrified Spiders

Like Newt Saliva and Witch's Butter, Petrified Spiders may be used in many a potion and spell. 'Tis not ideal to require the petrification of a familiar, of course, but alas—many sacrifices shall be required of thee should thou choose to pursue power and everlasting beauty. And remember thee well—a petrified spider proveth more delicious than a fresh one. A delightful crunch, ha!

1. Preheat the oven to 400°F.
2. Empty the can of chickpeas into a strainer to drain, then rinse with water.
3. Pour the chickpeas into a medium bowl along with the olive oil, garlic powder, sea salt, pepper, and paprika.
4. Spray a cookie sheet with cooking spray and spread the chickpeas in a single layer over the surface.
5. Bake until the chickpeas are crispy, about 15 to 20 minutes.
6. Serve warm.

SERVES
8

PREP TIME
25 minutes

COOK TIME
20 minutes

1 pound large-shell pasta

1 tablespoon olive oil

10 ounces extra-sharp cheddar cheese

8 ounces gruyère cheese

½ cup plus 2 tablespoons unsalted butter, divided

½ cup all-purpose flour

3 cups half-and-half

⅓ cup Italian seasoned bread crumbs

salt, to taste

pepper, to taste

Magicae "Mac"-xima

Ahh, yes, the Power Spell. The witch or parent who uses this recipe shall be all powerful, as no little one can resist the lure of mac 'n' cheese. But be ye warned—doomed as well is the witch who uses this spell, as it may come to pass that littles will request this and only this for every meal to come.

Adding broccoli is an easy way to make this spell just as powerful but a little more nutritious (in case it does end up on the short list of favorite spells).

1. Bring a large pot of salted water to a boil.
2. Add the pasta and cook al dente according to the package directions.
3. Drain the pasta in a colander and pour it into a 12-inch cast-iron skillet.
4. Add the olive oil, toss, and set aside.
5. While the water is boiling, grate the cheddar and gruyère cheeses. Combine and set aside.
6. In a medium saucepan, melt ½ cup butter over medium heat.
7. Add the flour to the butter and whisk well until fully combined.
8. Add the half-and-half, salt, and pepper, and whisk well until the mixture simmers.
9. Lower the heat to low and add the grated cheese in batches, mixing well after each addition so the cheese fully melts. Continue until only about a third of the cheese is left.
10. Pour the cheese mixture over the pasta in the cast-iron skillet and mix well.
11. Sprinkle the bread crumbs over the top of the pasta.
12. Cut the remaining 2 tablespoons butter into thin slices and distribute over the top of the pasta. Sprinkle on the remaining cheese.
13. Bake in the skillet for 20 minutes, or until the cheese on top is melted and slightly browned.

SERVES
10

PREP TIME
10 minutes

2 cups chopped
plum tomatoes

½ red onion, chopped

½ yellow onion, chopped

2 cloves garlic,
finely chopped

2 or 3 jalapeño peppers
(depending on your preferred
level of spiciness), diced

2 tablespoons fresh lime juice

⅓ cup chopped fresh cilantro

1 teaspoon ground cumin

¼ teaspoon salt

Burning Rain Salsa

This concoction is more than "but water," though it may not be exactly refreshing. Too many jalapeños, and it just might make fire in your hand (or mouth).

Burning Rain Salsa makes the perfect complement to the Full Moon Quesadilla (page 32), the Shush Ke Baby Tacos (page 54), or the Veggie Egg Cups (page 18).

1. Add all the ingredients except the salt to a food processor or blender. Pulse until you have your desired consistency. (A few quick pulses will result in a chunkier salsa, while blending more will produce a smoother, more liquid salsa). Stir in the salt.

2. Cover and refrigerate for at least 1 to 2 hours to allow the flavors to combine.

> **TIP:** For a milder salsa, remove the pith and seeds from the jalapeño before dicing. If you prefer a little more spice, leave them in.

Desserts & Treats

SERVES
8

PREP TIMES
5 minutes

½ cup (1 stick) unsalted butter, at room temperature

1 (8-ounce) package cream cheese, softened to room temperature

¼ cup powdered sugar

¼ cup light brown sugar, packed

1 teaspoon vanilla extract

¼ teaspoon salt

1 cup semisweet mini chocolate chips

Eye Cream Cookie Dip

This "eye cream" cookie dip might not make you look younger, but it will certainly make you feel younger—especially if you happen to be a millennial parent who fondly remembers Dunkaroos. It's just the right amount of sweet, and even though it doesn't have children's souls already mixed in, it's a perfectly youthful snack.

1. To the bowl of a stand mixer, add the butter, cream cheese, powdered sugar, brown sugar, vanilla, and salt. Using the paddle attachment, mix on low until smooth, about 2 to 3 minutes.
2. Using a rubber spatula, gently fold in the chocolate chips.
3. Transfer to a small bowl and serve with dippers of your choice, such as pretzels, apple slices, graham crackers, strawberries, or wafer cookies.

Sandy's Caramel Apples

SERVES
8

PREP TIME
10 minutes

COOK TIME
40 minutes

8 tart apples, such
as Granny Smith

8 wooden chopsticks
(optional)

1 cup (2 sticks)
unsalted butter

2 cups light brown
sugar, packed

1 cup light corn syrup

1 (14-ounce) can sweetened
condensed milk

2 teaspoons vanilla extract

toppings of choice, such
as sprinkles, candies,
mini marshmallows,
or chopped nuts

There's a reason why caramel apples are a classic fall snack! They are the perfect combination of sweet and tart, and they're endlessly customizable with toppings. Little ones will love decorating their own. And making them at home means you don't have to wait in an endless carnival stall line or—even worse—buy a prepackaged one from Walgreens. If you've never had a caramel apple, get ready—it'll change your life. Promise.

1. Wash and prepare your apples. Dip whole apples in boiling water and dry with a paper towel if the skins feel waxy after washing. Remove the stems and push a chopstick into the top of each apple—or cut the apples into slices for easier eating, if preferred. Line a baking sheet with parchment paper.

2. In a medium saucepan over medium-high heat, stir together the butter, brown sugar, corn syrup, and condensed milk. Bring to a boil while stirring constantly, then lower the heat to medium.

3. Cook, stirring constantly, for 25 to 30 minutes, or until a candy thermometer registers 248°F. At this point, drop a small bit of the caramel into a glass of cold water—it should form a small, firm ball when the caramel is ready. Remove from the heat and stir in the vanilla.

4. Quickly dip each apple (or slice) into the caramel, as high up the sides as you like but leaving at least ½ inch uncoated at the top.

5. Place on the parchment paper, decorate with toppings if you wish, and let cool. Refrigerate to store.

SERVES
8

PREP TIME
10 minutes

COOK TIME
1 hour 20 minutes

1 cup (2 sticks)
unsalted butter

2 cups gently crushed
unsalted pretzels

2 cups boiling water

1 (6-ounce) box
strawberry Jell-O mix

20 ounces frozen strawberries

1 cup granulated sugar

1 (8-ounce) package
cream cheese, softened
to room temperature

2 cups Cool Whip

Blessed Birthe Day Gelatin

If kids have an older sibling who is turning 16 (and may or may not receive their powers), then this Jell-O mold is the perfect birthday dessert for the younger sibs to help make. While Jell-O may not be en vogue right now, back when it was invented in (apparently) the 1690s, it was all the rage. When paired with a large, adorable spider, this dessert will make the perfect birthday gift for a young possible-witch. Plus, it jiggleth!

1. Preheat the oven to 400°F.
2. Melt the butter in a small saucepan over low to medium heat.
3. Mix the crushed pretzels with the melted butter in a small baking dish. Bake 10 minutes. Remove from the oven and let cool.
4. Boil water. When boiling, carefully measure 2 cups into a large bowl. Add the Jell-O mix and use a whisk to mix together well. Stir until the Jell-O dissolves, then refrigerate for about 20 minutes.
5. When the Jell-O just starts to get firm, stir in the strawberries. Pour the mixture into a fluted pan or a plastic mold and put in the refrigerator.
6. Mix together the sugar and cream cheese. Fold in the Cool Whip with a spatula.
7. Remove the Jell-O mold from the refrigerator and spread the cream cheese mixture over the top. (This will become the bottom when the mold is flipped over.) Then top the cream cheese mixture with the crushed pretzels.
8. Refrigerate until the mold is completely set, approximately 1 hour. To remove the Jell-O from the mold, turn the mold upside down onto a serving platter. Gently lift the mold so the Jell-O slides out onto the platter.

SERVES
4

PREP TIME
15 minutes

COOK TIME
20 minutes

4 glass jars (mason
or pint jars about 5
inches tall are ideal)

4 wooden skewers

4 clothespins

2 cups water

6 to 7 cups granulated
sugar, plus more for
coating the skewers

½ teaspoon flavoring oil

2 or 3 drops food coloring,
as needed (preferably green,
red, and/or purple!)

Fully Charged Crystal Candy

Anyone who is "really into" witchcraft or crystals should get ready for a really fun recipe. Part science experiment (or magick!) and part tasty candy treat, these rock candy crystals are as fun to grow as they are to eat.

While this recipe takes some time to make, once you have your candy crystals there's no need to wait for a full moon. They come fully charged with delicious, sugary magic, ready to harness—or create—some boundless energy!

1. Clean the glass jars thoroughly with hot water.
2. Wet the 4 wooden skewers with water and roll in granulated sugar. Set the skewers aside to dry on a paper towel.
3. Boil the water in a medium pan over medium-high heat. Add the 6 cups sugar a cup at a time, stirring after each addition. Let the sugar dissolve completely each time before adding more. Once all the sugar is dissolved, remove the pan from the heat.
4. Pour the mixture into a medium bowl. Add the flavoring oil and, if needed, food coloring to achieve the color you want. (Some flavoring oil may color the sugar syrup by itself.) Stir to evenly distribute.
5. Let the sugar syrup cool for 20 to 30 minutes.
6. Rinse and swirl the jars with hot water, then dump out the water.
7. Pour the sugar syrup into the 4 jars so it is evenly distributed. Then lower a skewer into each jars so it hangs ¾ inch above the bottom, and in the middle of the jar. Secure it by clipping it with a clothespin and resting the clothespin on the rim of the jar.
8. Place the jars in a cool place away from light and cover them with plastic wrap.
9. Crystals should form in 2 to 4 hours. If they don't, wait up to 12 hours and check again. If there is still no change, boil the syrup again, adding an additional cup of sugar. Repeat steps 6 through 9.

10. When the rock candy grows to your desired size (this may take a few days!), use a spoon to break the top layer of crystals and remove the candy from the jars. Transfer to an empty jar or cup so that it hangs as it did in the sugar syrup, clipped with the clothespin. Let the rock candy dry for 2 hours. Store in an airtight container for up to 6 months.

SERVES
8

PREP TIME
15 minutes

COOK TIME
50 minutes

4 pounds apples, peeled and sliced (Granny Smith, Honeycrisp, and Golden Delicious are good choices)

½ cup granulated sugar

½ cup light brown sugar, packed

⅓ cup all-purpose flour

1 teaspoon ground cinnamon

½ teaspoon allspice

¼ teaspoon ground nutmeg

¼ teaspoon sea salt

Pie Crust (page 88)

3 tablespoons unsalted butter

whole milk and sugar, for topping the crust

Poisoned Apple Pie

Nothing says fall quite like apples, in any form—eaten freshly picked, dipped in chocolate or caramel, or baked into this delicious pie. A word to the wise: people won't eat this if you tell them it's poisoned, so don't be an amateur—let them know so you'll have more for yourself!

This recipe provides instructions for homemade pie crust, but it's also easy to use a store-bought swap for this dish.

1. Preheat the oven to 375°F.
2. Peel, core, and cut the apples into thin slices.
3. In a large bowl, combine the apple slices, granulated and brown sugar, flour, cinnamon, allspice, nutmeg, and sea salt.
4. Roll out one ball of the pie crust dough on a cold, lightly floured surface. Roll from the center outward, using gentle but firm pressure, and place in a pie plate. Trim the edges if they hang too far over the edge of the plate.
5. Transfer the apple pie filling into the pie shell. Dot with butter.
6. Roll out the second dough ball and use a paring knife to cut a cat face out of the dough (you can mostly use triangles—2 on top for the ears, 2 horizontal diamonds for eyes, and an upside-down triangle for a nose—and slits for the whiskers). Place the dough over the pie filling. Fold the edges under the edges of the bottom crust and either pinch them together or use a fork to press them together.
7. Brush the top of the pie crust with milk and sprinkle with sugar. Cover the edge of the pie crust with aluminum foil.
8. Bake the pie for 25 minutes. Then remove the foil and bake for another 20 to 25 minutes, until golden brown. Serve warm.

2½ cups all-purpose flour

1 teaspoon salt

6 tablespoons (¾ stick) unsalted butter, chilled and cubed

¾ cup vegetable shortening, chilled

½ cup ice-cold water

Pie Crust

1. In a large bowl, mix together the flour and salt. Add the butter and shortening and blend together using a pastry cutter until it forms small pebbles.

2. Drizzle in the cold water, 1 tablespoon at a time, and stir with a wooden spoon. Stop adding water when the mixture begins forming large clumps.

3. Transfer the mixture to a floured work surface and lightly knead (with floured hands) until the butter and shortening are fully incorporated. The dough should not feel sticky.

4. Form the dough into two equal balls and flatten each of them into a disc about an inch thick. Wrap each disc tightly in plastic wrap and refrigerate for at least 2 hours.

Witches' Buttercream Cake Pops

SERVES
24

PREP TIME
15 minutes

COOK TIME
3 hours

1 box vanilla cake mix, plus the ingredients called for on the box

1 cup Buttercream Frosting (page 90)

24 ounces white chocolate candy melts

24 lollipop sticks

sprinkles or other decorations, if desired

Styrofoam block or cardboard box with holes poked in (for drying the pops)

Witches' butter is an essential ingredient in a power-giving spell. If your devil book doesn't specify, it is better to err on the side of unsalted butter! Keep salt as far away from a witch as possible.

Similarly, you'll want to stick with unsalted witches' butter for frosting these cake pops. Once your pops are formed and frosted, feel free to decorate them however you wish—with colored frosting, sprinkles, and so on. You could dress yours up as cutesy pumpkins or mummies, or even use candy eyeballs as an homage to dear booooook.

1. Preheat the oven as directed on the cake mix box. Mix the cake ingredients and bake according to the instructions on the box.
2. Remove the cake from the oven, transfer it to a cooling rack, and let it cool completely.
3. In a medium mixing bowl or the bowl of a stand mixer, crumble the cake and then add the frosting. Using the mixer's paddle attachment or a wooden spoon, blend until the frosting is fully combined with the cake crumbs and the mixture resembles wet sand.
4. Use a cookie scoop or teaspoon to form individual portions, using your hands to roll each one into a ball shape. You should end up with about 24 portions.
5. Place the balls on a cookie sheet lined with wax paper and refrigerate for 1 to 2 hours.
6. Take the balls out of the refrigerator and insert a lollipop stick into each one, pushing it about halfway through the ball.
7. Melt the white chocolate candy melts according to the package instructions.
8. One at a time, dip the cake balls into the melted candy. Make sure to swirl them around to coat the entire area.
9. Dip or roll the candy-coated balls in sprinkles, or decorate as desired.

10. Allow the pops to dry smoothly by placing the end of each stick into the Styrofoam block or box so the pops are raised into the air. Allow about an hour for the coating to set. Store in an airtight container in the refrigerator until you're ready to serve.

MAKES
2 cups

PREP TIME
20 minutes

½ cup vegetable shortening

½ cup (1 stick) unsalted butter, softened

1 teaspoon vanilla extract

4 cups sifted powdered sugar

2 tablespoons milk

pinch of salt

food coloring, if desired

Buttercream Frosting

1. In a large bowl, use a mixer on medium speed to cream together the shortening and butter until light and fluffy (about 1 or 2 minutes). Beat in the vanilla extract.

2. Add the powdered sugar about a cup at a time, mixing thoroughly after each addition. Make sure to scrape the sides of the bowl. When all the sugar is mixed in, the icing should look stiff.

3. While continuing to mix, drizzle in the milk until the icing reaches the desired smooth and fluffy consistency. Mix in the pinch of salt and food coloring, if using, until the icing is evenly colored.

SERVES
24 cookies

PREP TIME
30 minutes

1 cup Buttercream Frosting
(see page 90)

yellow food coloring

24 fudge-bottom cookies,
such as Keebler fudge
stripes cookies

24 peanut butter cup candies

24 small orange candy-
coated chocolates
(such as M&Ms)

Puritan Hat Cookies

Salem, Massachusetts, may not have been the peak of fashion in the 1600s, but these Puritan hat cookies are the peak of deliciousness, and very cute. While '90s kids know that every fashion trend will eventually come back around, we hope these hats reappear only as delightful confections and that the hat buckles, high socks, and winged shoes remain in history's vault.

You can use the making of this recipe as a way to introduce the history of Salem and the context behind the sisters' origin story. Older kids may be curious to understand what exactly is going on in those opening scenes of Hocus Pocus. Otherwise, just enjoy a marvelously easy little treat!

1. Unwrap the candies and set aside in a bowl.

2. In a small bowl, mix the vanilla frosting with 2 or 3 drops of yellow food coloring. Mix thoroughly, adding more food coloring 1 or 2 drops at a time until you reach your desired color. Scoop the frosting into a piping bag or sealable plastic bag with a small hole cut from the corner (about the size of a pencil tip).

3. Place the cookies fudge side up on a flat surface, such as a clean counter or a cookie sheet. Pipe a thin line of frosting around the outside of the wider end of a peanut butter cup. Place on top of the cookie, frosting side down. Repeat for all the cookies and peanut butter cups.

4. Pipe a thin line of frosting around a peanut butter cup where it meets the cookie (like a ribbon around the hat). Gently press a candy-coated chocolate into the frosting to look like the buckle. Repeat for all your cookies.

> **NOTE:** If you want to make your cookies from scratch, you can make a simple chocolate biscuit cookie. You can also use the sugar cookie dough from the Witches' Hat Cookies (page 94); use a round cookie cutter then dip them in melted chocolate.

SERVES
24 cookies

PREP TIME
1 ½ hours, including chill time

COOK TIME
10 minutes

3 cups all-purpose flour, plus more for dusting the dough ball

1 teaspoon baking powder

½ teaspoon salt

1 cup (2 sticks) unsalted butter, softened

1 cup granulated sugar

1 tablespoon milk

1 large egg

1 teaspoon vanilla extract

Witches' Hat Icing (page 95)

Witches' Hat Cookies

Knead the dough and roll it flat,

Trim the edge into a hat.

Dye the icing black as black,

And frost like this....

1. Add the flour, baking powder, and salt to a large bowl. Whisk until well blended.

2. Combine the butter and sugar in a separate large bowl. Using a hand mixer, beat until fluffy.

3. Add the milk, egg, and vanilla to the butter mixture and beat well.

4. Now add the flour in small portions, beating well after each addition.

5. Shape the dough into a large ball, lightly flour, then wrap in plastic wrap. Refrigerate for at least 1 hour.

6. Preheat the oven to 350°F. Line two baking sheets with parchment paper.

7. Lightly flour a work surface. Place a rolling pin in the middle of the dough ball and roll it forward once and backward once. Then flip the dough over, turn it 90 degrees, and roll again. Repeat this process until the dough is about ⅛-inch thick.

8. Cut your cookies using a cookie cutter shaped like a witch's hat. Then form the dough scraps into a ball and roll out again. Repeat this process until all the dough has been used.

9. Arrange the cookies on the parchment-lined baking sheets and place in the freezer for about 10 minutes.

10. Bake the cookies for 8 to 10 minutes, or until lightly golden. Let cool completely on a cooling rack before frosting.

11. To frost the cookies, scoop the icing into a plastic sandwich bag. Use scissors to snip the tip off one corner, making a hole only about the size of a pencil tip.

12. Gently squeeze icing around the cookie edges to outline the entire shape. Then use the frosting to fill in the shape completely. Let the cookies sit for about 30 minutes to let the icing settle and harden. Once the frosting has set, you can transfer the cookies to an airtight container to store them.

Witches' Hat Icing

3 ounces pasteurized
egg whites

1 teaspoon vanilla extract

4 cups powdered sugar

black, orange, and
purple food coloring

1. In the bowl of a stand mixer, combine the egg whites and vanilla. Beat until frothy.

2. Gradually add the powdered sugar, beating on low speed until the sugar is fully mixed in and the mixture is shiny. Turn the speed up to high and beat until stiff peaks form, about 5 to 7 minutes.

3. Separate the frosting into bowls for different colors. Add food coloring a couple of drops at a time to each bowl; stir in gently. Keep adding more drops until you have your desired colors.

SERVES
12

PREP TIME
20 minutes

COOK TIME
8 hours

3 envelopes unflavored
gelatin (.75 ounce total)

1 cup water, divided

1 ½ cups granulated sugar

1 cup light corn syrup

¼ teaspoon salt

1 teaspoon vanilla paste

orange gel food coloring

powdered sugar, for dusting

Homemade Halloween Marshmallows

Are homemade marshmallows the easiest recipe in this book? No. But are they good for you? Also no. They are, however, lots of fun for kids to make, and just complex enough to make you feel really successful when your kitchen magick turns out just right.

These marshmallows are the perfect complement to the Hot Chocolate Brew on page 110. Best of all, they're so deliciously sweet that even a handful of teenagers running amok will happily accept them as candy toll payment.

1. Combine the gelatin and ½ cup water in a small bowl and whisk with a fork. Let sit for 5 minutes.
2. Meanwhile, combine the sugar, corn syrup, salt, and ½ cup water in a small saucepan and cook over medium heat. Stir gently until the sugar dissolves.
3. Turn the heat to high. Cook the syrup until it reaches 240°F, using a candy thermometer to measure the temperature.
4. Pour the dissolved gelatin into the bowl of a stand mixer, making sure there are no clumps of undissolved gelatin. Attach the whisk attachment, set the mixer on low speed, and slowly pour in the sugar syrup until it is dissolved in the gelatin mixture. Then turn the mixer speed to high and whip the mixture until it is thick, about 5 minutes.
5. Add the vanilla paste and orange food coloring and mix thoroughly.
6. Using a sieve, generously dust an 8 x 12-inch nonmetal baking dish with powdered sugar. Pour the whipped mixture into the pan, using a rubber spatula to smooth the top. Dust with more powdered sugar. Cover and let stand overnight.
7. When the marshmallow mixture has dried out, turn the baking dish upside down over a cutting board to release the contents. Cut into squares, then dust with additional powdered sugar.

SERVES
4

PREP TIME
20 minutes

COOK TIME
20 minutes

1 ½ cups whole wheat
pastry flour

1 cup all-purpose flour

½ cup light brown sugar

1 teaspoon baking soda

½ teaspoon salt

½ teaspoon ground cinnamon

½ cup (1 stick) cold butter

¼ cup honey

¼ cup water

1 teaspoon vanilla extract

1 cup marshmallow creme

12 ounces semisweet
chocolate chips

2 tablespoons canola oil

In the Light of the Moon Pie

Without the moon, we would never see the success of the Black Flame Candle or be able to charge up our crystals. We wouldn't be able to summon witches from underground or see them backlit as they fly across the sky. And without a full moon, how would the weirdos know when to go out? Nothing is more mystical and witchy than the moon, and nothing is more retro than a moon pie. So here we pay homage to lunar magic with a tasty treat kids will "moon" over.

1. Preheat the oven to 350°F. Line 2 baking sheets with aluminum foil or parchment paper.

2. In a medium bowl, combine the flours, brown sugar, baking soda, salt, and cinnamon. Stir until blended well.

3. Cut the butter into ½-inch-thick pieces, then use a pastry cutter to blend the pieces into the flour mixture. Continue until the mixture comes together into a ball about the size of an apple and is well coated in the flour mixture.

4. Add the honey, water, and vanilla. Mix gently until dough is formed.

5. Flour your work surface and place the dough on the floured surface. Use your hands to form it into a ball. Continue working the dough with your hands until there are no remaining dry bits of flour.

6. Cut the dough in half and roll out one half to approximately ¼-inch thickness. This should allow you to cut approximately 8 dough circles, about 2⅓ inches in diameter. Place the dough rounds onto one of the lined baking sheets.

7. Repeat with the remaining half of the dough.

8. Transfer to the oven and bake for 10 to 12 minutes, or until very lightly golden. Remove from the oven and let cool on the pan for 2 to 4 minutes, then transfer to a cooling rack to cool completely.

9. Spread marshmallow cream on the flat side of a cookie and top with another cookie to form a marshmallow sandwich; repeat for the rest of the cookies. Place the cookie sandwiches in the freezer until the marshmallow sets, at least 20 minutes.

10. Melt the chocolate chips in a double boiler or in the microwave. Add the canola oil and stir continuously until smooth.

11. Drop each marshmallow cookie in the melted chocolate and use a fork to spoon the chocolate to cover all sides. Remove carefully (using 2 forks to lift the cookie gently is helpful) and place on a lined baking sheet. Let the chocolate fully set before serving.

SERVES
12

PREP TIME
2 minutes

COOK TIME
10 minutes

2 tablespoons vegetable oil

about 1 cup unpopped popcorn kernels (enough to make 7 quarts popcorn)

salt, to taste

1 cup salted roasted almonds

1 cup salted roasted cashews

1½ cups craisins (dried cranberries)

1 cup dark chocolate chips

Witch Fuel Popcorn

The quest for eternal youth and beauty can really take a toll. How can one be expected to stay up all night chasing brats around Salem when you haven't done a lick of cardio in more than 300 years? If you find yourself in need of a snack, grab a bit of this Witch Fuel. The popcorn and nuts will give you the protein and carbs you need, and the dark chocolate will give you a zip of caffeine, making this the perfect snack for a witch on the go.

1. Heat the vegetable oil in a large wok or saucepan over medium heat.
2. While the oil is heating, place 3 unpopped kernels of corn in the pot and cover with a lid.
3. When the kernels pop, add the rest of the popcorn kernels, place the lid back on top, and remove from the heat.
4. Holding the lid tight, gently shake the pot for about 30 seconds.
5. When the kernels start to pop, return the pot to the stove over medium heat.
6. As the kernels continue to pop, lift the pot [occasionally?] and gently shake it to keep kernels from remaining stationary on the bottom and burning.
7. When you hear fewer than three pops per second, turn off the heat, remove the pan from the stove, and keep shaking until the popping stops completely.
8. Quickly pour the popped kernels into a large bowl and salt to taste.
9. Add the almonds, cashews, craisins, and dark chocolate and stir to mix well.

SERVES
6

PREP TIME
10 minutes`

COOK TIME
35 minutes

2 large eggs

2 (6-ounce) containers plain whole-milk yogurt

1 yogurt container of sugar

1 teaspoon vanilla extract

1 yogurt container of vegetable oil, plus more to grease pan

4 yogurt containers of all-purpose flour

1½ teaspoons baking powder

sprinkles (preferably green, purple, and red, if you can find them)

Blood Orange Glaze (page 103)

Drop of an Enemy's Blood Orange Yogurt Cake

Don't you just love it when a recipe calls for blood oranges? They're so much more dramatic and thematic than regular navel oranges, and if you're interested in giving a recipe just that little bit of extra flourish, swapping in a blood orange is the way to go. Need a garnish for a drink? A deep red blood orange will take your breath away. How about a fresh summer salad? The reddish purple and orange flesh would stop any witch in her tracks, but especially a 300-year-old witch with a penchant for drama.

In this recipe, the blood orange makes for a delightfully zesty icing for a traditional yogurt cake that French witches have been making with their little morsels for ages. Even the littlest hands can help with this recipe, as all the ingredients can be measured out using the yogurt container!

1. Preheat the oven to 375°F.
2. Grease a 9-inch round baking dish with vegetable oil.
3. Crack the eggs into a medium bowl and beat with a fork or wire whisk. Add the yogurt, sugar, vanilla extract, and oil and gently stir to combine with the eggs.
4. In a separate bowl, mix the flour and baking powder. Add to the wet mixture and gently combine (don't overmix). Add however many sprinkles you want and gently combine.
5. Pour the mixture into the greased baking dish and bake for 35 minutes. The cake is fully cooked when a toothpick poked into the center comes out clean.
6. Slice, drizzle the pieces with the Blood Orange Glaze, and serve warm.

Blood Orange Glaze

zest of 1 blood orange

1½ cups powdered sugar

2 tablespoons freshly
squeezed blood orange juice

1. Mix the orange zest, powdered sugar, and orange juice in a small bowl, stirring vigorously until fully combined.

Krispy Rice Booooooks

PREP TIME
10 minutes

COOK TIME
20 minutes

3 tablespoons unsalted butter

1 (10-ounce) package of marshmallows

6 cups crispy rice cereal

12 White Milk Chocolate Hershey's Kisses

1 tube black or brown cake-decorating icing

These books may not have been bestowed by strange and ridiculously beautiful witches in a dark wood, but since they're treats meant for children, that is definitely a good thing. Like a magical tome containing powerful and evil spells, these treats will tempt anyone from young magicians to "clever white witches."

You can get as cute or as ugly as you desire with your decorations, but remember that all great boooo—ooo-ooooks have all-seeing eyes.

1. Place the butter and marshmallows in a microwave-safe bowl and heat on high in the microwave for 2 minutes. Stir, then microwave for another minute. Stir until smooth.

2. Add the crispy rice cereal to the melted marshmallows and stir with a wooden spoon until evenly mixed.

3. Coat a 13 x 9-inch pan with cooking spray. Evenly press the marshmallow mixture into the pan, using a buttered spatula or wax paper. Let cool completely.

4. Once cool, cut into 12 rectangles, 2 x 3 inches each. Press a white chocolate candy, point-down, into the right side of each rectangle.

5. Cut the tip of the icing tube. Squeeze the tube gently to make eyelashes for the candy eyes, scars, or other decorations.

SERVES
8

PREP TIME
2 minutes

COOK TIME
10 minutes

1 cup milk or dark
chocolate chips

1 teaspoon vegetable oil

16 pretzel rods

16 candy corns

Black Flame Candle Pretzels

These black flame candle pretzels probably don't have the power to bring witches back from the dead, but they definitely have the power to tame a hungry witch. On the off chance there's an unknown power enchanting your kitchen, maybe don't be an airhead and make them on a full moon night—if the wrong person takes one, who knows what sort of chaos may be set in motion!

1. Line a baking sheet with parchment paper.
2. Boil water in the bottom of a double boiler.
3. Place the chocolate in the top of the double boiler along with the vegetable oil. Set over the boiling water.
4. Stir constantly with a rubber spatula until the chocolate is melted and creamy, then remove from the heat.
5. Dip the top half of each pretzel rod in the melted chocolate, then place on the parchment-lined pan. Stick a candy corn to the top of each pretzel rod.
6. Using a teaspoon, drizzle more chocolate over the pretzels to add texture.
7. Place in the refrigerator until the chocolate hardens, at least 30 minutes. Store in the refrigerator until you're ready to serve.

Drinks

SERVES
2

COOK TIME
10 minutes

- 2 cups whole or 2% milk
- 5 teaspoons unsweetened cocoa powder
- 1 tablespoon maple syrup
- mini marshmallows or Homemade Halloween Marshmallows (page 97)

Hot Chocolate Brew

This recipe is perfect for when you just want to spend a quiet evening at home. Brew up a batch of homemade hot chocolate and settle in for a family movie viewing. For a more complex potion, use the recipe for Homemade Halloween Marshmallows to add on top!

1. Combine the milk and cocoa powder in a small saucepan over medium heat.
2. When the milk is warm but not yet boiling, add the maple syrup.
3. Stir with a whisk until the mixture comes to a boil.
4. Once boiling, reduce the heat to low and let simmer for 5 minutes.
5. Pour the hot chocolate into mugs, add mini or homemade marshmallows, and enjoy!

Eldest Sister's Seltzer

SERVES
4

PREP TIME
5 minutes

1 cup (8 ounces) lime juice

½ cup (4 ounces)
simple syrup

1 ½ cups (12 ounces)
seltzer water

lime slices for garnish.

Having siblings can be as difficult as it can be joyful, particularly when the brunt of planning and leading (or scheming) falls to one in particular. An oldest sibling can probably relate to many (though hopefully not all!) of our leading lady witch's hurdles in shepherding her younger sisters. When being the brains behind it all becomes a bit too much, an elder sibling may enjoy a quiet moment alone, or one-on-one with a parent, sipping this yummy lime rickey.

1. Mix the lime juice and simple syrup in a 2-cup measuring cup.
2. Fill 4 highball glasses with ice. Divide the lime-syrup mixture among the glasses.
3. Top off each glass with the seltzer water, garnish with lime slices, and serve.

NOTE: To make your own simple syrup, mix equal parts sugar and water in a saucepan and bring to a boil on the stove top, stirring, until the sugar is dissolved. Let cool.

SERVES
2

PREP TIME
5 minutes

COOK TIME
1 hour 10 minutes

2 cups granulated sugar

2 cups water

1 cup quartered fresh strawberries

1½ cups lemon lime soda

lime slice or strawberry, for garnish

Middle Mary's Mocktail

Middle children have it rough! It can be hard to find your place when everyone is jockeying for position. Who is the brains? Who the beauty? Am I more than just the super smeller of the litter? These are questions pondered over a lifetime, not just an afternoon, but start with a beverage break and a tasty Strawberry Citrus Fizz. Maybe you'll find you're the chef of the bunch!

1. In a medium saucepan over medium-high heat, slowly bring the sugar and water to a boil until the sugar is completely dissolved.
2. Remove the sugar syrup from the stove top, add the strawberries, and let steep for an hour. Remove the strawberries from the syrup using a slotted spoon and set aside.
3. Fill 2 highball glasses with ice. Add the lemon lime soda and top off with a drizzle of the strawberry simple syrup.
4. Garnish each glass with a lime slice or some of the strawberries.

SERVES
3

PREP TIME
5 minutes

COOK TIME
1 hour 40 minutes

6 cups water, divided

½ cup granulated sugar

¼ cup honey

3 tablespoons dried culinary lavender

12 lemons

purple food coloring

lemon slices or a sprig of lavender, for garnish (optional)

3 Jelly Belly gummy rats, for garnish

Luring Lavender Lemonade

Boys (and girls) will love this drink! If you have mischievous little imps who love rat tails, pretty spiders, and dancing around in the woods, they may feel a kinship with the inspiration behind this Lavender Lemonade. Sweet and just a little sour, this is a perfect refreshment after an afternoon of playing and will lure little children into the kitchen. The gummy rats are optional but will certainly add a little bit of drama.

1. Add 2 cups of the water and the ½ cup sugar to a small saucepan and set over medium heat until the water boils and the sugar is dissolved.

2. Remove from the stove and stir in the honey and 3 tablespoons dried lavender. Let steep for 1 ½ hours.

3. Cut the lemons in half and juice them into a bowl.

4. Strain the steeped liquid into a pitcher. Add the lemon juice and the remaining 4 cups of water.

5. Add food coloring until you achieve the color you want. Add lemon slices and lavender petals to the pitcher to garnish.

6. Pour over ice in water glasses and garnish each with a lucky rat tail from a gummy rat.

SERVES
10

PREP TIME
5 minutes

1 (0.13-ounce) packet
Kool-Aid unsweetened
lemon-lime powder mix

1 cup granulated sugar

2 cups pineapple juice

4 cups water

1 liter ginger ale

½ quart (2 cups) lime sorbet

lime slices, for garnish

Life Potion

While the best way to stay young and beautiful probably includes a peaceful mind, gratitude, and exercise, we mortals can't always tick all those boxes. So for the days when you're feeling a little more "old spinster sisters," convince your kiddos to help you mix up this life potion. The Kool-Aid is sure to bring you back to your childhood in the best way and give a little shot of nostalgia-laced pep to your step!

Don't worry, no children will be harmed in the making of this life potion, unless you count a little bit of elevated blood sugar!

1. In a large punch bowl or pitcher, whisk together the lemon-lime Kool-Aid powder, sugar, pineapple juice, water, and ginger ale.
2. Place 1 scoop of the sorbet into each of the highball glasses.
3. Pour the punch over the sorbet, garnish each glass with a lime slice, and serve.

SERVES
10

PREP TIME
10 minutes

COOK TIME
4 hours 15 minutes

9 assorted apples

1 orange

3 cinnamon sticks, plus
more for garnish

1 whole nutmeg

2 teaspoons whole cloves

½ teaspoon whole allspice

3½ quarts (14 cups) water

¼ cup (about 10 teaspoons)
light brown sugar, packed

Cider Spell

One cool autumn night when the moon is high

This warm apple potion will elicit a sigh.

A quiet evening at home, your cov'n will beg

For a mugful of apples, allspice, and nutmeg.

1. Core and cut the apples into ¼-inch wedges.
2. Cut the unpeeled orange crosswise into circular ¼-inch slices.
3. Put the apple and orange slices, 3 cinnamon sticks, nutmeg, cloves, and allspice into a slow cooker. Pour in the water, leaving half an inch space between the top of the water and the top of the slow cooker.
4. Cover and cook on high heat for 3 hours.
5. Remove the lid and use a potato masher to mash the apples in the slow cooker. Then cover and cook for 1 more hour.
6. Strain the contents of the slow cooker into a large pitcher using a mesh sieve. Then use a fine mesh strainer to press the juice out of the apple mash to add to the pitcher.
7. Add the brown sugar and stir until dissolved.
8. Serve the warm cider in a mug with a cinnamon stick garnish in each serving.

SERVES
1

PREP TIME
5 minutes

4 ounces (½ cup)
lemon lime soda

3 ounces (⅜ cup)
fresh peach juice

1 teaspoon grenadine

Peach slice for garnish

Peach Sunrise

Most witches aren't early birds. A beautiful morning sunrise will make them sick, as mortals, by the passage of time and those offensively chipper bird songs. As not-quite-immortals, the sunrise means they're dust, toast, pudding.

But if you're not a witch, you can enjoy this peach punch at any time of day, whether you're an early riser or a late-night mischief maker.

1. Fill a glass with ice, then add the lemon lime soda.
2. Pour the peach juice over the lemon lime soda; do not stir.
3. Slowly drizzle the grenadine over the top of the drink.
4. Garnish with the peach slice.

Conversions

VOLUME

U.S.	U.S. Equivalent	Metric
1 tablespoon (3 teaspoons)	½ fluid ounce	15 milliliters
¼ cup	2 fluid ounces	60 milliliters
⅓ cup	3 fluid ounces	90 milliliters
½ cup	4 fluid ounces	120 milliliters
⅔ cup	5 fluid ounces	150 milliliters
¾ cup	6 fluid ounces	180 milliliters
1 cup	8 fluid ounces	240 milliliters
2 cups	16 fluid ounces	480 milliliters

WEIGHT

U.S.	Metric
½ ounce	15 grams
1 ounce	30 grams
2 ounces	60 grams
¼ pound	115 grams
⅓ pound	150 grams
½ pound	225 grams
¾ pound	350 grams
1 pound	450 grams

TEMPERATURE

Fahrenheit (°F)	Celsius (°C)	Fahrenheit (°F)	Celsius (°C)
70°F	20°C	220°F	105°C
100°F	40°C	240°F	115°C
120°F	50°C	260°F	125°C
130°F	55°C	280°F	140°C
140°F	60°C	300°F	150°C
150°F	65°C	325°F	165°C
160°F	70°C	350°F	175°C
170°F	75°C	375°F	190°C
180°F	80°C	400°F	200°C
190°F	90°C	425°F	220°C
200°F	95°C	450°F	230°C

Recipe Index

RECIPE INDEX

Acknowledgments

As always, thank you to the team at Ulysses Press for making this book possible, for sharing my love of '90s movie references, and for believing that more people than just me watch *Hocus Pocus* multiple times every fall. And thank you to the team at Pacific & Court for all their support and for helping to make my last book a legit bestseller (!!) and helping readers connect with it.

Then, of course, massive thanks to Andrew, who is both the Mary and the Sarah to my Winnie, providing support, suggesting a calming circle when I skew toward drama, and helping to execute my schemes even when he's not particularly passionate about them.

Thanks to Beatrice, who has no idea I wrote this book but who provided the inspiration, the silly smiles, and—sometimes—the taste tests I needed to get through it. Hopefully one day soon she will be able to enjoy the *Hocus Pocus* movies with me, and one day after that she will realize I wrote this book and will be more proud of her mom than embarrassed by her.

To Disney+: thanks for providing a wider audience for HP, and finally giving us what we've wanted for nearly 30 years—not just one, but *two* musical numbers.

To Jeff, Reba, Alex, and Emily—thanks for being there with me in the good ole '90s.

Thanks to Beatrice again, for showing me the moon.

And thanks to Andrew again, because always.

About the Author

Bridget Thoreson is a writer and booklover based in Brooklyn, New York. She is the author of *USA Today* bestseller *The Unofficial Hocus Pocus Cookbook* and *XOXO: A Cocktail Book*, and a consulting author for *Are You My Wine?* Clearly, Bridget is very interested in drinking, eating, and pop culture.